LEARNING RESOURCE CENTER
Columbia Adventist Academy
11100 N.E. 189th Street
Battle Ground, WA 98604

TECHNOLOGY IN TIMES PAST

Ancient Rome

ROBERT SNEDDEN

A⁺

Smart Apple Media

Smart Apple Media is published by Black Rabbit Books
P.O. Box 3263, Mankato, Minnesota 56002

U.S. publication copyright © 2009 Black Rabbit Books. International copyright reserved in all countries. No part of this book may be reproduced in any form without written permission from the publisher.

Printed in the United States

Library of Congress Cataloging-in-Publication Data
Snedden, Robert.
     Ancient Rome / Robert Snedden.
     p. cm. — (Smart Apple Media. Technology in times past)
     Includes bibliographical references and index.
     Summary: "Covers the inventions and technology of the Ancient Roman Empire and how their ideas influenced technology today"—Provided by publisher.
     ISBN 978-1-59920-297-6
     1. Technology—Rome—History—Juvenile literature. 2. Rome—Civilization—Juvenile literature. I. Title.
T16.S65 2009
609.37—dc22

2007045676

Designed by Helen James
Edited by Pip Morgan
Illustrations by Graham Rosewarne
Picture research by Su Alexander

Picture acknowledgements
Page 7t Marco Cristofori/Corbis, b Vanni Archive/Corbis; 8 Guenter Rossenbach/Zefa/Corbis; 9 Arcaid/Corbis; 10 Massimo Listri/Corbis; 11 Mimmo Jodice/Corbis; 13t Guenter Rossenbach/Zefa/Corbis, b Bill Ross/Corbis; 14 Bettmann/Corbis; 15 Mimmo Jodice/Corbis; 16 Araldo de Luca/Corbis; 17 Morley von Sternberg/Arcaid/Corbis; 18 Free Agents Ltd/Corbis; 21t Jose Fuste Raga/Zefa/Corbis, b Sandro Vannini/Corbis; 22 Erich Lessing/AKG Images; 23 Fine Art Photographic Library/Corbis; 25t Adam Woolfitt/Corbis, b Richard Cummins/Corbis; 26 Erich Lessing/AKG Images; 27 Richard Hamilton Smith/Corbis; 28 Eye Ubiquitous/Corbis; 29 Museo Della Civilta Romana Rome/ Gianni Dagli Orti/The Art Archive; 30 Araldo de Luca/Corbis; 31 Bruce Adams; Eye Ubiquitous/Corbis; 33t Joseph Martin/ AKG Images, b Anders Ryman/Corbis; 34 Araldo de Luca/Corbis; 35 Museo Della Civilta Romana Rome/Gianni Dagli Orti/The Art Archive; 36 Araldo de Luca/Corbis; 37t James L. Amos/Corbis, b Macduff Everton/Corbis; 38 Erich Lessing/AKG Images; 39 Owen Franken/Corbis:

Front cover Eye Ubiquitous/Corbis

9 8 7 6 5 4 3 2

CONTENTS

THE GLORY OF ROME

Rome today is one of the world's great cities, with a history that stretches back nearly 3,000 years. For several hundred years, it was the center of an enormous empire, which extended from Britain in the northwest to present-day Iraq in the east. More than 65 million people lived within this empire—around a fifth of the entire world population at the time.

A BUSTLING CITY

At the height of the empire, Rome was a bustling city of a million people. No other city in the world approached that size until the Industrial Revolution 1,500 years later, which began a great period of growth in many European cities.

Rome needed an efficient transportation system to supply its people's needs: housing, food, and a regular supply of fresh water for drinking and sanitation. As Rome grew in power, a massive

MILLIONS OF SLAVES

The ancient Romans had no real need to find mechanical ways of doing things, such as constructing buildings, because they had a huge number of slaves to do the work for them. According to some estimates, there were as many as ten million slaves in the empire.

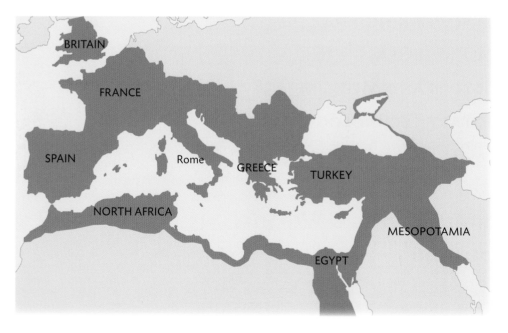

This map shows the Roman Empire at its greatest extent in about A.D. 117.

construction program widened streets, tore down and replaced abandoned buildings, and erected bridges to span the Tiber River. Aqueducts fed water into the city to supply homes, bathhouses, and fountains.

SUPERB ENGINEERS

The architects of Imperial Rome were not only concerned with the day-to-day needs of the city, but also with building great works, such as the Colosseum, the Forum, the Pantheon, and the Circus Maximus—a huge racetrack for chariots watched by 250,000 people.

This book shows the role that technology played in the running of the Roman Empire and in the daily lives of the people who lived there. Though the Romans were superb engineers, they were not great inventors. A great deal of the technology the Romans depended on was borrowed from other civilizations, such as the Greeks, then adapted and often improved.

Among the ruins of the Forum in Rome, you can see the Arch of Septimus Severus and the remaining columns of the Temple of Saturn and the Temple of Vespasian.

The Pantheon in Rome is a grand temple that was built by Emperor Hadrian in the 2nd century A.D.

7

BUILT TO LAST

The most popular building material used by the early Romans was mud brick strengthened by timber. Later, they began to use large blocks of stone held together by mortar. The real breakthrough in Roman building came when they discovered how to make concrete.

CEMENT AND CONCRETE

Concrete is still widely used in construction today. Many people think of it as a modern invention, but the Romans got there first.

During the 2nd century B.C., the Romans discovered that mixing together lime and a volcanic ash called pozzolana with seawater resulted in an unusually strong cement that set as hard as stone when it dried. It was also waterproof, so it was ideal for bridge building. Adding gravel and stones to the cement produced concrete.

Concrete was the ideal material for building on a grand scale. It was cheaper and stronger than stone, so the Romans used it instead of traditional materials. After a great fire devastated Rome in A.D. 64, the city was largely reconstructed with concrete.

The Colosseum in Rome (opposite) was a huge arena that was built largely of concrete and held a crowd of 55,000 people.

Concrete blocks were mainly used in building The National Theater in London.

CONCRETE CONSTRUCTION

One of the advantages of concrete was that it could be poured into timber frameworks. Builders erected walls in stages. They made wooden frames to hold the first layer of concrete in place at ground level. They built up bricks or stones on either side to form a cavity into which they shoveled wet concrete.

Scaffolding allowed them to build the higher parts of the wall. Layers of stone placed between the layers of concrete gave extra strength and stability. Concrete vaults and domes were used in ever more daring ways in palaces, temples, bathhouses, and other public buildings. The builders often faced concrete walls with bricks or smooth stone.

WOODWORK

Roman carpenters used many tools, such as chisels and saws, that carpenters today would recognize. They had no screws for woodworking, so they joined pieces of wood with various joints. They carried out neat and accurate work with different-sized chisels. They used an adze, a downward-pointing blade attached to a curved handle, to trim rough timbers and shape and smooth their surfaces.

WOOD SAWS

The Romans introduced several improvements to the carpenter's saw. Previously, saws only cut when they were pulled through the wood, so the Romans made a saw that they could push as well as pull. They also invented the frame saw, in which the blade was attached to wooden uprights joined to a crossbar. Some frame saws were quite large and had to be operated by two people.

The Comforts of Home

Wealthy Romans lived in lavish townhouses with many rooms, but poorer people lived in a single room in a crowded apartment block. Most of these blocks of apartments were badly constructed and offered little in the way of home comforts.

Domus, Sweet Domus

A wealthy Roman and his family lived in a house called a *domus*. (*Domus* means "house" or "home.") These houses were generally two-story buildings made of red brick with tiled roofs. The rooms were arranged around a central courtyard or garden called an *atrium*. The members of the household relaxed on balconies overlooking the *atrium*.

A few of the wealthiest households had a special luxury: they had glass fitted in their windows, especially in the colder northern parts of the empire. The Romans may have been the first to use glass for this purpose.

Decorating with Mosaics

The floors and walls were often decorated with mosaics. These were patterns or pictures made from *tesserae*: small cubes of stone, glass, pottery, or tile. A layer of fine mortar was spread over the floor or wall. While it was still damp, the *tesserae* were pressed in to build up the picture, like putting together the pieces of a jigsaw puzzle. When the mosaic was complete, the pieces were smoothed and polished. Some were completed section by section in a workshop, then assembled on site.

Under-Floor Heating

The Romans invented central heating and called it a *hypocaust*, which means "heat from below." The floors of a large house were

Mosaics were important features of wealthy Roman homes. This mosaic is in the Ambassadorial Hall of the Quirinal Palace in Rome.

This ruined courtyard was once a part of the House of Neptune and Amphitrite at Herculaneum.

SANITATION

Only the wealthiest could afford to connect their *domus* to a water supply. Rainwater was collected in a pool in the courtyard, called an *impluvium*, and stored in a cistern. This water was used for cleaning rather than drinking. Some people had a private bath within the *domus*, and perhaps a bathroom near the *atrium*. But most used chamber pots that were emptied into cesspits.

supported above a low cellar on stacks of clay tiles. Hot air from a furnace, also used for heating water, was fed into the cellar through arched gaps in the walls. This heated the floor of the room. Flues in the walls allowed the warm air from the cellar and the smoke from the furnace to rise up and escape beneath the eaves of the house.

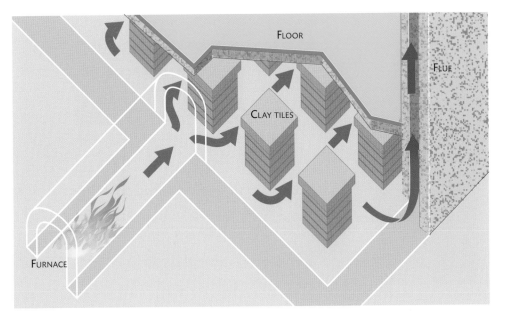

FLOOR

FLUE

CLAY TILES

FURNACE

A hypocaust works by channeling hot air (red arrows) under the floor of a room. Warm air and fumes (blue arrow) escape up through a flue.

ARCHES AND DOMES

Most of the ideas in Roman architecture came from ancient Greece, but Roman architects and engineers had two advantages over the Greeks. One was their invention of concrete and the other was their mastery of the art of building arches.

ARCH-BUILDING

Arches are strong, attractive, and very useful. They are a trademark of Roman architecture. Until Roman times, most entrances into buildings had two upright posts with a stone called a lintel laid across the top. The size of an entrance was limited by the weight of the lintel—if it was too heavy, it cracked in the center and broke into pieces. The invention of the arch meant that entrances could be much wider. Arches were made with smaller, lighter, wedge-shaped blocks of stone that pressed firmly together. The curved shape of the arch spread the weight of the stone blocks around the arch and onto the supports, but not through the center of the arch.

Arches require much less material than a solid wall of the same height, so they enabled the Romans to build impressive bridges, as well as the aqueducts that carried their water.

DOME OF THE GODS

Mastery of the arch allowed the Romans to build domes. A dome may be thought of as a series of arches, each sharing a center. The largest and best-preserved dome from the ancient world is the Pantheon, the shrine of all of the gods, in Rome. The building that survives today was completed between A.D. 118 and

KEYSTONE

The Romans built arches in several stages. They used wooden scaffolding to support the structure before they put the keystone in place.

LEARNING RESOURCE CENTER
Columbia Adventist Academy
11100 N.E. 189th Street
Battle Ground, WA 98604

TRIUMPHAL ARCHES

The Romans erected more than 30 triumphal arches to celebrate their military victories. Only a few of these great monuments survive today. Triumphal arches have been built in modern times, too. For example, the Roman Arch of Titus inspired the Arc de Triomphe, which was built in Paris in the early 19th century.

The Emperor Septimius Severus built a triumphal arch in Rome in A.D. 203.

125, during the time of the Emperor Hadrian. The dome is an almost perfect hemisphere. It is 138 feet (42 m) across and 72 feet (22 m) high. A 26-foot (8-m) circular opening at the center of the roof lets light into the building —a revolutionary idea for the time.

The dome was built from layers of concrete mixed with lightweight volcanic rocks such as pumice. Brick arches may have supported the concrete's weight while it set and were then later removed. The dome weighs more than 5,500 tons (5,000 t) and is supported on foundations more than 23 feet (7 m) thick. The lower walls were made of concrete mixed with a tough stone called *travertine*.

Until the 20th century, the Pantheon was the largest dome ever constructed.

Aqueducts

A healthy community needs a constant supply of fresh water. In small towns and in the countryside, people could take all the water they needed from streams and wells, but for a large city such as Rome, this just wasn't possible. The Romans needed a more sophisticated means of supplying water.

Water Supply

As early as 312 B.C., the Romans began to construct a system of channels and bridges to carry water into Rome from the surrounding hillsides. They were not the first to build these watercourses, or aqueducts. An aqueduct 31 miles (50 km) long was built around 400 years earlier to carry water to the city of Nineveh in Assyria. India, Egypt, and other countries also built aqueducts before the Romans.

Although they were not the first, the Romans were undoubtedly the best. Their engineers combined tunneling, pipe laying, bridge building, and reservoir construction to create a water supply system that was second to none in the ancient world.

Tunnels and Channels

To ensure a steady flow of water, engineers cut tunnels at precise angles through the

The Romans built this aqueduct (opposite) to bring water to their city of Nemausus. It is now called the Pont du Gard and is near Nîmes, France.

A Gentle Slope

Aqueducts relied on gravity to move water from a distant source. Just as a stream flows down a hillside, so the water gradually moves along the aqueduct. The Aqua Claudia, built in A.D. 47, supplied Rome from a source that was just 820 feet (250 m) higher than Rome itself. Water flowed down a gentle slope as the aqueduct dropped only three feet (1 m) in height for every 918 feet (280 m) of its 43-mile (70-km) length.

mountains. Where water was taken across a valley, it was directed through a stone channel carried above the valley on a series of arches. The Aqua Claudia runs over a 6-mile (10-km) series of arches on its way to Rome. A stone roof covering the aqueduct channel protected the water from contamination by poisons, garbage, and ash.

Holding Tanks

When the aqueducts reached the city, they emptied into three holding tanks. One supplied the public drinking fountains, while the second supplied the public baths. The third tank provided the water for Rome's wealthier citizens, who could afford to have water supplied directly to their homes.

The Trevi Fountain in Rome was built in 1762 and stands at the end of the Aqua Virgo, an aqueduct completed in 19 B.C.

A Lot of Water

About 160 million gallons (600 million L) of water were delivered daily to Rome by aqueducts. More water per person flowed into ancient Rome than into present-day New York.

Keeping Clean

Once water from the aqueducts reached Rome and settled into the holding tanks, it was directed to different districts through a network of large lead pipes. Smaller pipes made of lead, wood, or terra-cotta fed the water into public fountains, bathhouses, and the homes of the wealthy.

The Public Baths

The Romans were very interested in cleanliness, and they built public baths for the citizens of every large town in the empire. Several Roman emperors, including Augustus, Nero, and Diocletian, had great public baths built in Rome. These magnificent structures were richly decorated with sculptures and mosaics. Most bathhouses followed the same general layout. First, there was the changing room, where the bather removed his clothes. Next, came the warm room, or *tepidarium*, the floor of which was heated by a *hypocaust* (see page 11). Then, there was an even hotter room, where the walls were heated, too. Here an attendant covered the bather's skin with olive oil and scraped it with a curved scraper called a *strigil* to remove dirt. After that, the bather might take a plunge in a cold pool before getting dressed again.

The Baths of Caracalla in Rome were once enjoyed by more than 1,600 bathers.

Bath Spa in the United Kingdom has been famous for its healing waters since Roman times. The baths are still used today and include the Minerva Pool (above).

SEWER SYSTEMS

Water from the aqueducts ran continuously, so an efficient drainage system was essential. Roman cities had a network of underground sewer systems. Surprisingly, the Romans did not make the connection between sewage and disease—they were really just interested in getting rid of the smells.

Rome's sewers and drains emptied directly into the Tiber River. The sewers carried not only sewage, but also drainage water and rainwater runoff. The sewer system probably took away at least as much water as came in on the aqueducts; the Tiber's flow was greatly increased by the additions from Rome's sewers. The main sewer, the Cloaca Maxima, still exists nearly 3,000 years after it was built.

FLUSHED AWAY

Most homes had little in the way of sanitation, but public bathrooms were plentiful. These were usually next door to the baths, but were not private.

Users sat shoulder to shoulder over holes on stone benches. Water from the baths ran through channels beneath the lavatory benches, flushing the waste away.

The Romans didn't have toilet paper. Instead, they used sponges on sticks, which they rinsed after use. Most people carried their own sponges with them. No one really liked the idea of using someone else's sponge.

ROAD-BUILDING

An empire as large as Rome's needs a good system of communication. Rome kept in touch with its provinces by means of its road network: goods were transported for trading; messengers carried information, instructions, and news; and soldiers moved swiftly to trouble spots.

A NETWORK OF ROADS

The Romans were great road builders. Their first major road was the Appian Way, a straight road begun in 312 B.C. to connect Rome with the town of Capua to the south. Later, it was extended to the port of Brindisi in the southeast. By the 4th century A.D., Roman engineers had constructed a remarkable network of more than 52,800 miles (85,000 km) of road stretching right across the empire.

ARMY ENGINEERS

Soldiers did most of the road-building. Roman armies came equipped with whatever they needed for the construction work, which surveyors and engineers organized.

The basic method of road-building was the same throughout the empire, although it varied according to the local conditions and the building materials that were available.

Paving stones cover the surface of the Appian Way.

To start with, the soldiers raised an embankment and shaped it so that rain water drained into ditches on either side. The embankment was at least 13 feet (4 m) wide, enough to let two vehicles pass. Engineers laid a foundation of larger rocks, followed by layers of smaller stones, gravel, and sand that were rammed down into place. Roads in towns and cities were often finished with a top layer of cobbles.

KEEPING IT STRAIGHT

Roman roads are famous for being straight. A surveyor used a *groma* to make sure a road was straight. This is a pole with two pieces of wood connected at right angles on top to make a cross shape. From each of the four ends of the cross, the surveyor suspended a weight on a line. He stood between a starting point and the place he wanted the road to go.

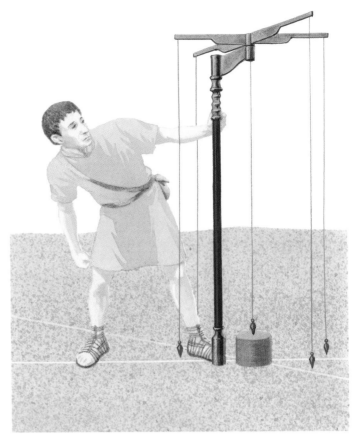

A Roman engineer uses a groma to make sure a new road is straight.

With the groma in the ground, he twisted the crosspieces until opposite strings lined up with the starting point and also with the point he was aiming for. He then knew that the starting point, where he was, and the next point were all in a straight line.

HERO'S DIOPTRA

Roman surveyors used a *dioptra* (left) to work out heights and angles. This tool had a gearing system that allowed the surveyor to turn the sights on a circular metal plate and align them with a sighting rod held some distance away. Hero of Alexander, known as the "Machine Man," invented the *dioptra* in the 1st century A.D. It is the forerunner of the theodolite that surveyors use today.

BUILDING BRIDGES

The Romans built some of the ancient world's finest bridges so that their roads could cross rivers. Their arch-building skills enabled them to build bridges with much longer spans than were possible using stone beams. Bridges with stone arches lasted longer than wooden ones, and many still stand after 2,000 years.

CRANES

Building a bridge of stone arches involves lifting heavy weights. For example, the magnificent Alcantara Bridge over the Tagus River in Toledo, Spain, has huge arch stones that weigh up to 9 tons (8 t) each. These arch stones were so accurately shaped that no cement was used to keep them together. The Romans used cranes to maneuver each stone into position in the 95-foot (29-m) spans that make up the bridge.

The Greeks had invented the crane in the 6th century B.C., but the Romans made many improvements during their huge construction programs. The Roman cranes didn't have powerful engines like our modern-day cranes. Instead, they used a system of pulleys, winches, and treadmills, powered by slaves. A large, treadmill-powered crane could lift 13,000 pounds (5,900 kg). But the engineers had other ways of lifting much heavier weights (see page 21).

Roman engineers erected cranes with a clever system of pulleys to help them lift heavy weights, such as stone blocks.

COFFERDAMS

The Romans devised an ingenious method for building a bridge across a river that had no islands or rocks where they could build supporting piers. This method was the cofferdam. First, the engineers drove two

Roman engineers built the arched Alcantara Bridge over the Tagus River in Toledo, Spain.

LIFTING HUGE STONES

The corner blocks of the temple to Jupiter at Baalbek in Lebanon weighed 110 tons (100 t) and were raised 62 feet (19 m) above the ground.

To lift such heavy weights into position, the Roman engineers set up a lifting tower. They surrounded it with a number of cylinders called capstans that can wind and unwind rope. Turning the capstans enabled a system of pulleys to raise the massive stone blocks.

concentric circles of wooden piles into the riverbed at the site where a pier was to be built. They wove wickerwork in and out of the wooden piles, then filled the gap between them with clay. This cofferdam kept the water out. Next, they pumped or bailed out the water inside the wicker-lined circles and exposed the riverbed. After digging out the silt and mud to expose the bedrock, they poured in pozzolana cement, which was waterproof, and then built the pier.

The Ponte Sant'Angelo bridge across the Tiber River in Rome was built using cofferdams. More than 1,800 years later, it still stands, a testament to the skill of the Roman bridge builders.

The Roman Emperor Hadrian built Ponte Sant'Angelo over the Tiber River between A.D. *134 and 139.*

TRAVELING BY ROAD

The Romans had a wonderful transportation network of roads and bridges. So how did they travel around on it? Many traveled by horse, but the Romans also had various wheeled vehicles —ranging from carts to two- and four-wheeled carriages—for moving themselves and their goods.

RIDING THE ROADS

Well-built Roman roads made getting from place to place easy and quick. Those who needed to move swiftly, such as the emperor's messengers, traveled by horse. Around the end of the 1st century B.C., Emperor Augustus set up a series of rest stations at intervals of 6 to 18 miles (10 to 30 km) along the roads. There, his couriers could be sure of finding food, water, and fresh horses, enabling them to travel up to 50 miles (80 km) in a day.

SADDLES, BUT NO STIRRUPS

The harnesses and saddles used by the horse riders of ancient Rome are similar to those used by riders today. However, they did not have stirrups. A Roman saddle had four corners, each with a horn. These four horns gave the rider firm support, so they did not need stirrups. The stirrup was invented in India during the 2nd century B.C., but it was nearly a thousand years before European riders adopted it.

This relief carving shows a raeda *pulled by a pair of horses.*

The four-wheeled coach pulled by a team of horses remained an important method of transportation for centuries. This Victorian painting is The Arrival of the Royal Mail, Brighton, England *by John Charles Maggs.*

CARTS AND CARRIAGES

For short distances, the Romans used a simple cart pulled by oxen. This was little more than a platform of boards attached to a set of solid wooden wheels. The axles were fixed rigidly to the wagon and the wheels were fixed firmly to the axles. This made the cart very difficult to steer.

Over long distances, passengers and freight were transported in a four-wheeled, covered carriage called a *raeda*. This was pulled by mules or horses, harnessed two abreast. Families traveling together often used a *raeda*. For overnight journeys, it could be fitted with hammocks.

A single traveler with little baggage could make a faster journey using the two-wheeled, uncovered *cisium*. Two horses, one between shafts and the other attached by traces, drew the *cisium*. It had a single seat that was broad enough for the passenger to sit alongside the driver. The *cisium* had no suspension, so the sensible traveler always remembered to take a few cushions along!

PEDESTRIAN PRECINCTS

By law, no vehicles were allowed on the streets of Rome for the first ten hours of the day to prevent congestion. There were a few exceptions. Market wagons bringing goods in at night could leave empty at first light. Wagons full of materials for public building works and chariots taking part in triumphal parades could also enter. The rules didn't last long because people complained about their sleep being interrupted by the goods wagons!

TRAVELING BY SEA

Much of Rome's trade was carried by ships. Moving large cargos by sea rather than overland was cheaper and easier. Flat-bottomed barges took goods up the Tiber and often ferried cargos from merchant ships that were too big to make the journey themselves.

BUILDING A SHIP

Roman shipbuilders laid down the keel and formed the hull out of carefully shaped planks of wood joined together, edge to edge, with mortise and tenon joints. Strengthening ribs were fitted inside this frame and the deck was built on top. The lower part of the hull was often treated with wax and tarred fabric to protect it from sea worms, a type of mollusk that bores into wood.

THE MERCHANT FLEET

The Roman merchant fleet was the largest in the world during the 2nd century A.D. The

A Roman merchant ship is moored beside a dock as a new cargo is loaded on board.

most common type of merchant ship was the *corbita*, which had a round hull and a curving prow and stern. *Corbitas* varied in size and could carry up to 385 tons (350 t) of cargo. They moved slowly, at little more than 3 knots, yet they traded as far away as India.

The biggest cargo ships carried grain from Egypt to Rome. The largest were 180 feet (55 m) long and 46 feet (14 m) wide, and carried more than 990 tons (900 t) of cargo

The ruins of a Roman lighthouse stand at Dover Castle, Kent.

GUIDING LIGHTS

Lighthouses at many Mediterranean ports guided ships in at night. In A.D. 50, the Romans built a lighthouse at Ostia, the nearest port to Rome, on an island created by filling the hulk of a ship with concrete. At first, they lit beacon fires on the tower, but after the 1st century A.D., they used oil lamps in lanterns that had panes made of glass or thin horn.

Lighthouses, such as Fastnet Rock, to the south of Ireland, are still important to the safety of ships and their crew.

and 1,000 passengers. They were rigged with square sails. Both the Romans and the Greeks used triangular sails called lateens on their smaller craft.

The Romans didn't build passenger ships, so travelers found space on a merchant ship that was heading in the right direction. There might have been a few cabins for more important passengers, but everyone else stayed on the open deck.

FINDING THE WAY

Roman sailors had no compasses to help them plot their journeys. The Chinese invention did not reach Europe until the 12th century A.D. Roman navigators either stuck to the coasts, keeping in sight of land, or they used the sky to guide them. For example, the height of the sun above the horizon at noon told them how far north or south they were.

Food and Farming

The staple food of the Romans was bread. They didn't know about rice or potatoes because these reached Europe many centuries later. Huge quantities of grain were needed to feed the empire's large population every year, so a successful harvest was very important. Much of this grain was imported from North Africa.

Working the Land

Roman farmers tilled the land and produced their crops using tools and agricultural techniques that hadn't changed much for centuries. They didn't need new and more efficient ways of working the land because slaves provided most of the labor.

Farmers used simple tools: they sowed wheat, barley, and corn seed by hand from baskets carried around their necks, and later they reaped the harvest with iron sickles. One improvement the Romans did make was to balance the weight of the sickle blade with the weight of the handle. As a result, the reaping sickle was easier to use.

Plowing

Before the farmers sowed their seed, they prepared the ground with a light plow. This was like a heavy pole pulled through the ground by a pair of oxen, and had been used for thousands of years. This plow worked well enough in the dry climates and light soils of the lands around

This Roman mosaic from the 3rd century A.D. shows a farmer plowing his fields with a pair of oxen.

the Mediterranean and the Middle East, but it was of little use on the heavy clay soils of Northern Europe's lowland plains.

The Romans adapted the plow to different conditions. In southern Italy, for example, they strengthened it by adding an iron plowshare—a cutting blade—to the tip of the pole. Sometimes they mounted the plow on wheels so that the person guiding the oxen could steer it more easily.

It may have been the Romans in Northern Europe who first had the idea of adding a coulter to the plow. This was a heavy blade that hung down in front of the plowshare, breaking up the soil and making it easier to plow. Another addition to the plow was a set of iron hooks, called an *irpex*, that tore out roots and weeds from the soil.

SEPARATING THE GRAIN

After the harvest, the farm workers separated the grain from the chaff (the unwanted parts of the plant). One method of doing this was to use a *tribulum*. This was a heavy wooden sled, drawn by oxen, that was studded on the

Modern farmers, such as this farmer in Illinois, plow their fields with a mechanized plow pulled by a tractor.

REAPING MACHINE

A reaping machine called a *vallus* was invented in Gaul (present-day France) but wasn't widely used. It had a closely spaced row of sharp prongs attached to the front of a frame. A donkey pushed the *vallus* along so that the prongs gripped the grain stalks. A hopper, like the grass box on a lawnmower, caught the heads of grain as they were thrown into the air.

bottom with nails or sharp stones for pressing the grain out of the chaff. Another method of separating cereals from their straw was the Punic cart, which came from North Africa. It had toothed rollers for pressing out the grain and was pulled by donkeys.

DAILY BREAD

The Romans spread their grain on a drying floor heated by a *hypocaust*, then stored it inside bins in granaries. The floors of these long narrow buildings were raised on wooden or stone supports to keep mice and rats out. The inner walls were sealed with a foul-smelling substance called *amurca* to deter rats and mice.

MAKING FLOUR

Before the grain was made into bread, it was ground into flour with heavy millstones that were usually turned by donkeys. The flour was rather coarse and had to be sifted using a sifter made of linen or horsehair. This device trapped the unground bits of grain and let the finer flour fall through into storage jars.

THE WATERWHEEL

One of the few examples of the Romans making use of an energy source, besides the muscle power of slaves, is the waterwheel. Vitruvius, a Roman architect and engineer, invented the waterwheel during the 1st century B.C. There were two types, the undershot wheel and the overshot wheel.

The undershot waterwheel was placed upright in the middle of a fast-flowing stream or river. The rushing water turned the paddles at the bottom of the wheel, which was linked to a millstone by a series of gears.

MIGHTY MILLS

The Romans built their largest water mill at Barbegal, France, around A.D. 300. Water from an aqueduct was carried along two streams, both of which flowed down eight levels. On each level, there was an overshot waterwheel driving a millstone, so there were 16 millstones in all. The Barabegal mills could grind enough grain in a day to feed 12,000 people.

The Romans constructed large wooden waterwheels called norias *on the Orontes River in Hama, Syria.*

This carving shows a Roman baker using a long pole with a flat end to remove hot bread from an oven.

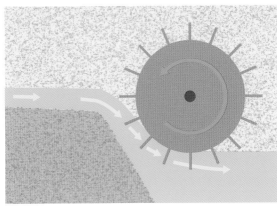

UNDERSHOT WATERWHEEL

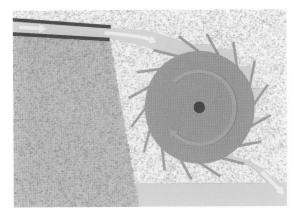

OVERSHOT WATERWHEEL

Flowing water strikes the paddles and turns the undershot and overshot waterwheels.

The overshot wheel was more difficult to build, but it could be used where water levels were low. Water was collected in a millpond, then directed through a channel to strike the paddles, which were set at an angle, at the top of the wheel. An overshot wheel was up to eight times more efficient than an undershot wheel.

BAKING THE BREAD

Most people relied on bakers because they did not have the means to make bread themselves. Some evidence suggests that the Romans invented a machine to knead the dough. Wooden paddles attached to a post were placed inside a container with the dough. A donkey turned the paddles, saving the baker the hard work of kneading. The bread was then baked in brick ovens, which were heated by a fire inside. When the oven was hot enough, the fire was raked out and the bread placed inside.

Clothing and Textiles

Most of the clothes the Romans wore were made of linen or wool. Linen came from flax and hemp plants, which were easy to grow and, like wool, were spun into cloth. Very wealthy Romans wore clothes made from silk imported from China.

This mosaic shows the clothes that wealthy Roman women wore.

Preparing the Fibers

Farmers usually sheared their sheep during the summer months using iron shears. They teased the wool by hand, then combed it to remove dirt and to smooth out the fibers. They spun the fibers with a wooden hand spindle, which was turned on the ground like a top to draw the fibers into a yarn. You can tell which part of the empire a piece of cloth came from by looking at the way the thread turns. People in the western provinces spun the spindle clockwise, whereas people in the eastern provinces spun it counterclockwise.

Growers harvested their flax and hemp in the summer, too. They soaked the plants in water to break down the tough outer parts, then dried out and beat the fibers with wooden mallets before combing out the fibers on a special combing board.

Weaving the Fibers

Many Roman households owned a loom on which they wove the fibers and made their own cloth. One of the more common types was the warp-weighted loom, which had two upright beams connected at the top by a bar called the cloth bar. Vertical threads, called

Modern looms, such as this one in a tartan factory, are mechanized so that large amounts of cloth can be made.

the warp threads, were hung from the cloth bar. The number of warp threads on the loom determined the width of the cloth: the greater the number, the wider the cloth.

Two sets of warp threads were kept apart by a rod running parallel to the cloth bar and tied to a weight at the bottom that stopped them from getting tangled. The thread that was being woven, called the weft thread, was passed back and forth between the warp threads until the cloth was completed. Wooden combs and the weaving sword, or *spatha*, pushed the weft threads up to create a tighter weave.

DYEING CLOTH

Wool was dyed as a fleece, as yarn, or when a garment was finished. Most often, the Romans dyed the wool after shearing and before spinning.

They may have occasionally dyed the wool before shearing. So you can imagine Roman fields full of crimson sheep!

Often, the undyed fibers were treated with alum or other chemicals that made the dye stick fast to the fibers. The Romans used animal dyes (see box below) and vegetable dyes, such as red madder (from a plant root) and brilliant yellow saffron (from autumn crocus flowers).

ROYAL PURPLE

The Romans collected a purple dye from a mollusk called *Murex brandaris*. Many thousands of shellfish were needed to get just a little of the dye, so it was very expensive. Julius Caesar and his successor Augustus Caesar decreed that only the emperor and his household were allowed to wear togas dyed with the rare purple.

Metals and Mining

The Romans used a number of metals, including silver, gold, lead, tin, and iron. They extracted these metals by mining their ores from the ground. If they could, they dug the ores out at the surface, but sometimes they had no choice but to dig down and follow a rich vein underground.

The Misery of Mining

Mining was usually done by criminals and slaves because the conditions were harsh. They dug narrow vertical shafts into the ground where the ore was located, then widened them into horizontal galleries where they removed the rocks containing the ore. The oil lamps they worked by used up the oxygen and made breathing difficult. Sometimes they dug additional parallel shafts to let warm air rise from the mine and allow cooler air in from outside.

Breaking up the Rocks

Removing rock from the mines was a difficult process. The miners heated rocks with fires, then doused them with vinegar when they were very hot. The sudden temperature change split the rocks, but the smell must have been unpleasant.

The miners usually broke up the rocks with iron tools, although they also used stone hammers and wedges. They broke hard stone with a pointed iron bar that they struck

A cross-section of a Roman mine shows slaves removing rock from a vein of ore (red) in a gallery. They entered and left the mine via a vertical shaft.

*Remains of a Roman mine can be seen
in the tunnels at Arditurri, Spain.*

Going Down

A Roman mineshaft could be about 650 feet (198 m) deep. Horizontal galleries were dug out sideways from the vertical shaft. These galleries were only 3 feet (1 m) wide and 3 feet (1 m) high, and could stretch for more than half a mile (0.8 km) as the miners followed the vein of the ore. Some tunnels in a mine may have been more than 1 mile (1.6 km) long.

with a hammer. They removed softer rock with iron picks that had curved blades. Often, the ore was carried to the surface in baskets and buckets. In larger mines, the ore was hauled up the shaft with a rope and a device called a windlass.

Flooded Mines

Flooding was a constant danger in the mines. Miners sometimes dug drainage channels or made slaves bail out the water. Some mines had a waterwheel with bucket-shaped paddles that were waterproofed with pitch or wax. Men turned the wheel like a treadmill so that the paddles scooped up the water and deposited it on a higher level. A series of wheels could lift the water from the lower mine workings to the surface. The Rio Tinto silver mine in Spain had eight pairs of wheels that could lift the water 100 feet (30 m).

Gold mining continues to this day at mines such as the Inti Raymi mine in Bolivia.

33

Metalworking

The Romans extracted metals from the ores they mined, then produced various useful things. Skilled craftsmen found ingenious ways of processing and shaping metal from the ores. The metals they worked with most were bronze and iron.

Bronze

Bronze was the most important metal of the ancient world before iron became available. Bronze is a mixture of different metals called an alloy. Roman craftsmen mixed copper, tin, and lead. There were probably nearly as many bronzesmiths as blacksmiths in the empire. Although more and more iron tools and weapons were produced, bronze had one big advantage: it could be melted and poured into molds, something the Romans could not do with iron.

Roman cooks used bronze pots and pans in the kitchen, people wore bronze belt buckles and brooches, and soldiers wore bronze armor. Figurines of athletes, military heroes, government officials, and gods were also made of bronze.

The Romans made many objects out of bronze, such as this oil lamp in the form of a winged horse.

Iron and Steel

Iron is harder and stronger than either bronze or copper. As a metal, iron had been in use for around a thousand years by the time of the Roman Empire. Knowledge of its uses probably spread from Greece, where it was used widely.

High temperatures are needed to extract iron from its ore. The Romans built charcoal-burning furnaces, using foot bellows to intensify the heat, but they still could not make the furnaces hot enough to produce molten metal. The best they achieved was a small ball of iron, called a bloom, which they removed by breaking open the furnace.

THE BLACKSMITH

Practically every town in the Roman empire had at least one blacksmith. He heated ingots of iron until they were red hot, then shaped them on an anvil with a hammer and pincers. The blacksmith made all kinds of pots, tools, and other items that the local people needed.

Foot bellows pumped air into the furnace, making the fire burn more fiercely. The higher heat helped to extract metal from the ore.

enough to melt it, so they could not pour it into molds to shape it. Instead, the metal workers hammered the iron into bars called wrought iron, which they were able to shape by further heating and hammering. So they could make things such as tools and buckles that were hammered out, but not objects that had to be cast, such as bells.

To make their iron stronger, the Romans reheated it between layers of charcoal. Charcoal contains carbon, which forms steel when mixed with iron. The highest quality blades with cutting edges for tools and weapons were made from steel. The secret of steel-making probably arrived from India. But when the Roman Empire came to an end, the secret was lost to Europe for nearly a thousand years.

This carving shows a Roman blacksmith hammering metal at his forge.

GOLD AND GLASS

Skilled craftsmen made and sold all kinds of goods from workshops in their homes. Some made household utensils from bronze, while others made lamps and jars from a type of pottery called terra-cotta. Iron was used to make rings, and an alloy of copper and zinc produced a cheap substitute for gold. Two important materials were gold and glass.

WORKING WITH GOLD

Gold is often found beside veins of quartz in the rock faces of mines. The Romans extracted it by hammering the rock, grinding it to a powder, and then running water over the powder. The lighter powdered rock was washed away, leaving the heavy gold behind. Sometimes the gold was naturally alloyed with other metals, such as silver or copper. These were removed by treating the gold with salt and sulfur. The pure gold was melted down and cast into blocks called ingots.

A goldsmith was a highly respected craftsman. He received gold in the form of ingots, from which he made sheet metal and wire that he turned into jewelry. To make sheet metal, he repeatedly hammered the ingot on a metal or stone anvil until it was very thin. By rolling a strip of gold between stone or bronze plates, he made wire. He had punches and stamps of various sizes for making patterns in the gold. He also had chisels, engraving tools, and tongs, and used burnishing stones to polish the metal. He had a charcoal fire with bellows to melt the metal when necessary.

Roman goldsmiths made beautiful jewelry, such as this gold earring with five pendants.

Roman glassblowers created a range of jars, vases, and bottles.

GLASSMAKING

People first discovered how to make glass in the Middle East, approximately 2,500 years before the Roman Empire. The ancient Egyptians were skilled at glassmaking, but the Romans improved it. They made glass by heating a mixture of silica (which comes from sand), soda, and lime in a furnace to drive off impurities. The mixture was then heated again in a clay dish, called a crucible, to temperatures of more than 2,000°F (1,100°C.) This produced molten glass.

GLASSBLOWING

Around 30 B.C., possibly in Syria, someone discovered that it was possible to shape molten glass by blowing air into it. The skill of glassblowing soon spread throughout the empire. Enormous numbers of glass objects were produced. They were used as drinking vessels, for storage, as cosmetics containers, and for the wealthy, as windows.

ARENA SOUVENIRS

After a day watching the games at an arena, spectators often bought a glass beaker as a souvenir, just as we might buy a T-shirt today. The beakers were decorated with pictures of popular gladiators. A beaker often showed a picture of the sporting event taking place that day as well as the names of the participants who were well-known to the fans.

A modern glassblower works on a piece at a factory in Orrefors, Sweden.

DOCTORS AND MEDICINE

A doctor in ancient Rome had little or no training. Most simply learned their skills as apprentices to other doctors. Many so-called doctors offered little more than prayers to the gods and magical incantations. They treated people on street corners or in their homes.

SURGICAL SKILLS

Roman doctors tackled some surprisingly delicate operations, such as removing small tumors and repairing a hernia. They even removed cataracts from the eyes. A cataract is a clouding of the lens that causes blindness if left untreated. The doctor inserted a thin needle inside a tube into the lens and broke up the cataract with it. He then removed the needle and sucked out the cataract fragments through the tube. Another method was to use the needle to push the cataract to the bottom of the eye out of the way.

The Roman army created hospitals where surgeons found new ways of patching up wounded soldiers, improving medical techniques in the process.

TOOLS OF THE TRADE

Roman doctors had an impressive array of medical instruments. Some would not look

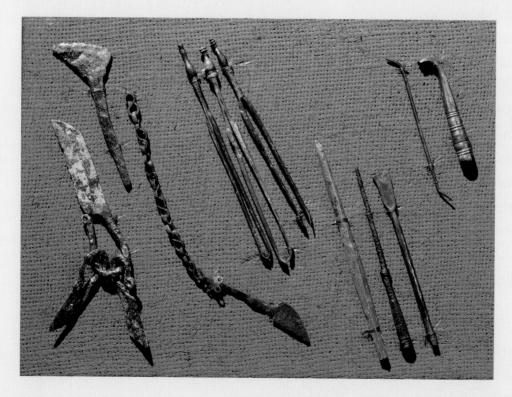

Roman doctors had a number of different surgical implements to help them perform medical operations.

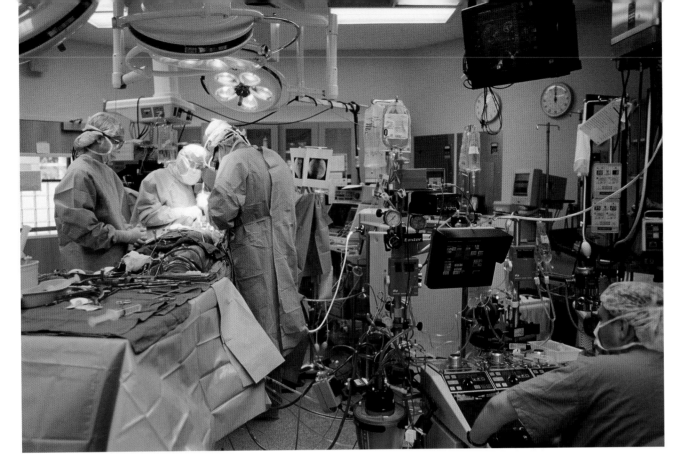

out of place in a modern operating room. They were often made from bronze, as this was a practical and relatively cheap way to produce surgical instruments, though the best doctors preferred instruments made from fine quality Austrian steel. Doctors commonly used a range of instruments, such as surgical scissors, scalpels, bone saws, and a variety of probes, hooks, and forceps.

DRUGS AND ANESTHESIA

Many ancient Roman medicines began as folk remedies and some were more effective than others. Many people were afraid of being poisoned and doctors could make a good living by supplying antidotes that were unlikely to do any good and might have been harmful. Occasionally, by luck, someone would stumble across something that worked.

The anesthetics that Roman doctors used were not nearly as effective or powerful as

As well as high-tech medical instruments, surgeons in modern operating rooms continue to use scalpels and anesthesia.

the ones we have today. Opium and other substances were often used to numb a patient, but the pain and discomfort of an operation must have been frightful.

A HOLE IN THE HEAD

One of the most extraordinary procedures carried out by Roman doctors was trepanation. This involved drilling a hole in a patient's skull. The Romans believed that this was a good way to cure headaches. Today, surgeons may use a similar procedure, called a craniotomy, during a brain operation.

MILITARY TECHNOLOGY

The Roman army was a formidable fighting force. Well-equipped and highly disciplined Roman soldiers brought vast areas of land under Roman rule. After conquering neighboring territories, the army then had to hold on to their conquests, rule the people, and keep the peace.

FORGING THE SWORD

The main weapon of the Roman soldier was the iron sword. The heated blade was hammered into shape by a blacksmith, then quenched by plunging it into water.

Quenching made the metal hard, but also made it brittle, so the blacksmith tempered the blade by reheating it. The blacksmith needed a great deal of skill to judge when the temperature was right to make a blade that would be both hard and sharp.

ANCIENT ARTILLERY

The Romans learned to use artillery from the Greeks. By the time of Julius Caesar in the 1st century B.C., the Roman army had become experts at laying siege to towns and cities. The army commanders had the finest artillery weapons of the time at their disposal, including large and powerful catapults.

One of the most impressive Roman weapons was the *ballista*. This Greek invention looked like a big crossbow

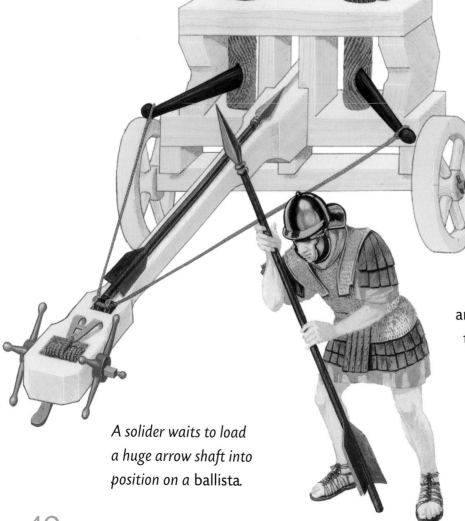

A solider waits to load a huge arrow shaft into position on a ballista.

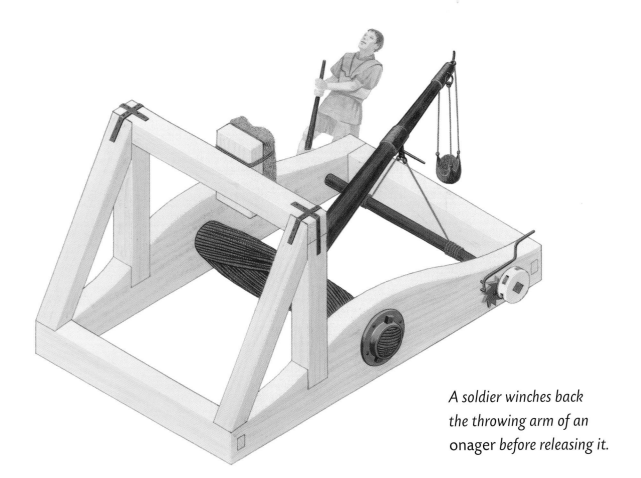

A soldier winches back the throwing arm of an onager *before releasing it.*

mounted on a tripod. The bowstring was connected to two separate arms, which were in turn attached to bundles of animal sinew, the tough cords that join muscle to bone.

A ratchet winched the bowstring back so that it could not spring forward before it was ready to fire. A heavy iron-tipped bolt was placed in a groove and the *ballista* was aimed and fired. It could propel the bolt 985 feet (300 m) with great accuracy.

Kick Like a Mule

The *onager* was a catapult that hurled rocks at defenders. Like the *ballista*, it was adapted from Greek technology and could hurl a 110-pound (50-kg) boulder a distance of 1,300 feet (400 m). It was named after the wild ass (the onager) because of the mighty kick it could give. A large stone was placed in the sling of the *onager's* throwing arm. The arm was held between twisted bundles

of animal sinew or rope. Then the arm was winched back and released, hurling the rock at great speed. *Onagers* were difficult to aim, but when they hit their targets they were very effective.

You're Surrounded!

In A.D. 67, the Emperor Vespasian and his Roman army laid siege to the city of Jotapata (Tel Yodfat in present-day Israel). He placed three legions, which were equipped with 160 artillery weapons, around the city. These pounded the walls and defenses with all kinds of bolts, stones, and burning materials. Eventually, after 47 days, the Romans captured the city.

ROMAN TIME LINE

753 B.C. The accepted date of the founding of Rome.

510 B.C. The foundation of the Roman Republic.

ca. 500 B.C. A Roman invents the first safety pin. The idea is lost with the fall of the empire and is not rediscovered until the 19th century.

312 B.C. Roman engineers begin work on the Via Appia, a road that will later be extended to the coast town of Brindisi. Work also begins on the first aqueduct to carry water into Rome. The Aqua Appia brings water from springs 10 miles (16 km) away.

290 B.C. Rome conquers central Italy.

ca. 280 B.C. The Romans begin to use coins.

272 B.C. The Aqua Anio aqueduct is built. It runs underground for most of its 40-mile (64-km) course.

264–241 B.C. The Romans wage war against the Carthaginians in North Africa. They build their first warships during this period.

206 B.C. Rome conquers Spain.

ca. 200 B.C. Concrete is used for the first time in the town of Palestrina. The first apartment buildings (called *insulae*), 3 stories tall, are built in Rome.

149–146 B.C. Carthage is destroyed and North Africa becomes a Roman province. Greece comes under Roman domination.

144–140 B.C. The Aqua Marcia is built. It is 57 miles (92 km) long and is the first aqueduct to have long sections carried on arches.

142 B.C. The first stone bridge is built over the Tiber River.

ca. 100 B.C. Five-story *insulae* are built in Rome. Engineers learn how to use arches to make domes. The first windows, in the form of glass skylights, are installed in a few wealthy homes. The Romans discover that adding the volcanic pozzolana ash to their concrete makes it strong and waterproof.

85 B.C. The *hypocaust* heating system is invented by Gaius Sergia Orata.

55 B.C. Julius Caesar's military engineers succeed in building a bridge across the Rhine River in just ten days.

49 B.C. Julius Caesar conquers Gaul (France).

27 B.C. The republic collapses and is replaced by the empire.

19 B.C. The Pont du Gard aqueduct in France is built.

A.D. 1 The engineer Vitruvius describes the first known undershot waterwheel.

A.D. 43 The Romans invade Britain.

A.D. 70 The Emperor Vespasian orders the building of the Colosseum. There will be no bigger theater in the world until the 20th century.

A.D. 79 The volcano Vesuvius erupts, burying the town of Pompeii under ash.

A.D. 117 The Roman Empire reaches its greatest extent.

A.D. 122–26 The Emperor Hadrian orders the building of a wall (Hadrian's Wall) that stretches across the Roman province of Britannia to protect it from attack by the tribes to the north.

A.D. 130 Hadrian builds the Pantheon, the shrine of all of the gods, in Rome.

A.D. 230 The last of the major aqueducts carrying water to Rome is completed.

ca. A.D. 300 The overshot waterwheel is developed.

A.D. 410 The Visigoths invade Italy, destroy Rome, and overrun Spain.

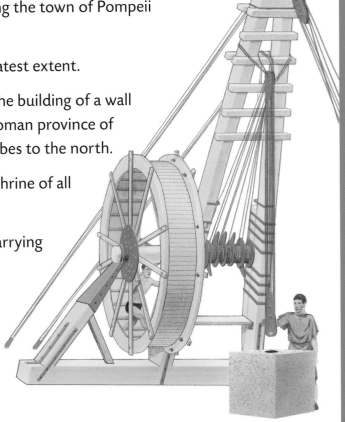

GLOSSARY

alloy A mixture of two or more different metals; for example, bronze is an alloy formed by mixing copper and tin.

anvil A heavy block of iron on which hot metals are shaped by hammering.

aqueduct A channel built to carry water from one place to another; the water flows down the channel by gravity.

bellows A device for producing a strong current of air to make a fire burn more fiercely.

cesspit A pit for collecting wastewater and sewage.

cistern An artificial reservoir for storing water.

concentric A term for circles that have the same center.

crucible A dish that can withstand high temperatures and be used for heating substances.

faced A wall that is faced has a decorative or protective covering.

flue A pipe used to lead smoke from a fire to the outside of a building.

granary A storehouse for grain.

hemisphere Half of a sphere.

hernia When part of an organ in the body emerges through a tear or a weakness in the muscle that surrounds it.

impurities Unwanted substances in a mixture.

Industrial Revolution The change in society brought about by the introduction of large scale industrial production of goods in factories using powered tools and machines; the Industrial Revolution began in England around 1760.

ingot Metal that has been cast into a bar for ease of shipping and storage.

keystone The central wedge-shaped stone at the top of an arch.

mollusk A type of invertebrate (an animal without a backbone), usually with a hard protective shell. Snails and oysters are mollusks.

mortar A mixture of cement, sand, and water used by builders to bind stone and similar materials.

pier A vertical support for the span of a bridge.

piles Long columns of timber driven into the ground to provide the foundations for a building.

Punic Relating to the ancient city of Carthage in North Africa. Carthage was destroyed by Rome in 146 B.C.

quartz A hard, shiny mineral formed from crystals of silicon dioxide; found in most rocks, especially granite and sandstone.

sanitation Keeping conditions clean and hygienic, especially to prevent the spread of disease.

sickle A tool with a short handle and sharp, curved blade used for harvesting crops by hand.

temper To toughen metal by heating it to a temperature below its melting point and then cooling it slowly.

theodolite An instrument used by surveyors to measure horizontal and vertical angles.

traces Side straps by which a horse is attached to the vehicle it is pulling.

FURTHER READING

Decker, Zilah. *National Geographic Investigates Ancient Rome: Archaeology Unlocks the Secrets of Rome's Past.* Washington, D.C. : National Geographic, 2007.

Dickinson, Rachel. *Tools of the Ancient Romans: A Kid's Guide to the History and Science of Life in Ancient Rome.* Norwich, Vt.: Nomad Press, 2006.

Hewitt, Sally. *The Romans. Starting History.* North Mankato, Minn.: Smart Apple Media, 2007.

Maynard, Charles W. *The Technology of Ancient Rome.* New York: Rosen Central Pub., 2006.

WEB SITES

Web Sites for Kids:
http://www.kent.k12.wa.us/staff/
DarleneBishop/rome/Rome.html
Learn more about some of ancient Rome's technological marvels, including the Roman Forums, the Colosseum, and the Roman Baths.

http://www.historyforkids.org/learn/
romans
See more pictures of Roman architecture and take a video tour of the Pantheon.

Web Sites for Teachers:
http://school.discoveryeducation.com/
lessonplans/programs/prosperity
These activities show students the influence that ancient Rome had on the world.

http://www.teach-nology.com/themes/
social/rome
This site is a valuable resource for lessons about ancient Rome, including hands-on activities, lesson plans, and worksheets.

Index